# Grandpa's Christmas:

## The Incredible Holy Supper of Christmas Eve

# Alvin Alexsi Currier

# Dedication and Acknowledgements

I dedicate these pages to the young of our Church, from toddlers to teens and beyond, who not only join us in keeping the faith, but also question us old ones about it. You bless us by asking and by God's grace may our experience be of some blessing to you.

I'd like to acknowledge my debt to my patient translators, especially Fr. Marek and Fr. Peter, and to all the cordial Baba's I interviewed in Wisconsin, Poland, Slovakia, and the Trans Carpathian Ukraine, who each in her own way explained to me the right way, to observe the 12-course meal of Christmas Eve. Thanks also to Sherri Ketz who got me started with her Mother-in-law's hand written instructions, Michael Riley who nursed me through the layout and publication, and of course, for the love and support of my wife Anastasia.

# Foreword

As the author of this book
and the old man
who drew the illustrations
I want to be clear,
right from the beginning,
that although I am a Grandfather,
I am not the Grandpa of this story.
He is my creation; born from worshipping
with the  descendants of emigrants
from the Carpathian Mountains of Europe
in a little Orthodox Church in the country.
For years I pondered how one of them
would answer his modern American grandchild
if asked about Christmas in the Old Country.
This amazing story is the result of that pondering.

So first of all this book is, the imagined answer
of a Grandpa from the Carpathian Mountains.
Secondly, it presents the heart of the feast
as I have come to treasure it, over a lifetime,
of reading, interviews, travels, and celebrations.
And finally this story is rooted in a real story
that I first heard over forty-two years ago.
I still cry now when I read it.

*Alvin Alexsi Currier*

The following books by Alvin Alexsi Currier
are available through the author's website:
www.AlvinAlexsiCurrier.com

The Miraculous Child, 1996

Aloysha's Apple, 1997

How The Monastery came to be
on the top of the Mountain, 1999

The Wonderful Life of Russia's Saint Sergius
of Radonezh, 2001

Old Maria, 2002

Grandma's Ritual Towel, 2011

The Blue Lady of Sycamore Hill, 2013

Grandpa's Icon, 2014

Karelia, The Songsingers' Land,
and the Land of Mary's Song. 1991 & 2016

# Grandpa's Christmas:

## The Incredible Holy Supper
## of Christmas Eve

# Alvin Alexsi Currier

It was from a prayer and a tear
      that I became clear
      what Christmas was all about.
   Let me tell you what happened
   so long ago when I was a boy
   in the wild Carpathian Mountains
   so far from here, across the sea,
   in the old world, from where we came.
We were the folk from the hills
and the majestic, mysterious mountains;
the offspring of settlers and refugees,
even fleeing serfs and sometime thieves,
seeking simply survival and freedom.
We lived by hard work and our wits.
Poverty and hunger were our enemies,
along with the winter, the wolf, and the bear.
      The freedom of our hidden highland homes
      made us as leery of the lowland lords
      as they were suspicious of how we  survived
      the dark and mysterious mountains.

On my papers I was called a Ruthenian,
and as an Austrian, my passport claimed me,
but for all of us the truth seemed to be;
our first allegiance was not to Vienna's Throne,
the Hungarian Crown or the Russian Tsar,
but to Christ our Lord, the King of Heaven.

2

The onion domes of our Orthodox churches
were the flags of our rugged realm
for our Kingdom was both of the heavens
and the forests, fields, and creeks
hidden among the valleys and peaks
of our beloved Carpathian mountains.
The languages we spoke
from wherever we came
slowly melted into a common tongue
rooted in our Churches' Slavonic.
But that's all history and geography.
It's all about maps, migrations, and family trees.
But to get to the place where I want to take you,
you can't travel by car, train, or airplane,
but with imagination, through time, you must fly
to those olden days of winters deep darkness,
when a vast stillness would cover the land,
and in isolated homesteads it was lonely.

Imagine no blinking lights or lit up stores,
no holiday specials, blaring carols, or TV graphics.
Imagine instead under star studded heavens
a crowded cabin with a flickering lamp,
where a mother softly hums while she's cooking
and the family is quite alone, for days and nights.

4

As a young boy I remember so clearly
that for Christmas that year
my uncle who'd gone to America
sent me a Kodak camera.
   Only years later did I remember
   the sorrowful pain of that December,
   for it was during the war
   and father was away at the front.
But then in the gathering dusk of Christmas Eve
we kids crouched by the window to see
who would be in the gathering night
the first the evening star to sight;
the star that would be the Christmas Star,
the star proclaiming Jesus' birth,
the star announcing peace on earth.
   Then by chance I gave a backward glance
   and froze in fear, as I saw a tear
   on my mother's cheek
   as she stood by the icon praying.
I turned quickly back to the darkening sky,
but what did I see?
Not a star in the heavens
but a man on the earth.
   "Mommy, mommy," I cried.
   "Come quick, come see.
There's a man on the road in the snow!"

Mother rushed to the window
and muffled a shriek
for clearly she saw
he was exhausted and weak.
She heaved up the bolt
pushed open the door
and an icy wind swooshed over the floor.
She cried to the man:
"In the name of God, come here, come here!"
But as he staggered slowly near
high in the sky I saw it so clear;
"Look, look." I yelled,
"The star is here."
Together we lifted our eyes to gaze
and together all our arms did raise
as we made the sign of the cross.
The strangers face grew strong and bright.
His voice like a trumpet pierced the night.
"Christ is born," he cried.
"Glorify Him," we replied.
Once more and louder he cried.
Again and louder we replied.
One more time in a rich rolling tone
his voice echoed out over the valley
as a chorus of stars blazed forth in the sky
echoing the glad reply:
"Glorify Him."

Suddenly we were cold
and crowded quickly into our cottage.
Warm wonderful smells swirled around us
and I confess that I was very hungry,
for all the daylong I'd had little to eat.
In fact from St. Phillip's day in November
we had kept a strict fast for Jesus' birth,
and we'd gone without dairy or meat,
but tonight, we would end our fast,
with a fabulous, fasting food feast.
   It was our people's way of saying
   -or our way of celebrating-
   that poor though we be,
   God through His love and creation
   gave us all of the gifts we needed
   for an abundant life and a fabulous feast.
With hunger I was eyeing a plate of Bolbalky,
   those luscious wee baked bread balls
   all glazed with honey and poppy seeds,
when my mother finished talking to the stranger,
and he laid a hand on my shoulder, and said,
"Tonight you must be the man of the house,
but I will help you. So go get your coat,
and the lantern, and we'll go to the barn."

Shocked but silent I wondered:
"but why to the barn?"
as I said, "Goodbye" to the Bobalky.

9

Our home was a building, both long and narrow
and our barn was the other end of our house,
but we went outside to get there.
When we entered the barn I was amazed.
The stranger greeted our horse and cow by name,
and while I was hauling fresh water,
our Old Bossy even let him milk her.
He knew where father had put away
the finest hay to save for this day,
and when I wondered to myself
why he was fussing so long in the barn
the stranger suddenly knelt before me
holding the Nativity icon.
Softly he said, "Look here, the icon is clear,
as the prophet Isaiah tells us:
'the ox knows its owner
and the donkey his masters manger.'
So first at the feast come creations creatures
for they were first to worship the King."

Since then I've always wondered how
that icon got in the barn and I've
never seen a manger scene without
seeing a donkey and an Ox hovering
over the Christ Child.

With a pail full of milk, and an arm full of hay
We returned from the barn to the cottage.
The table was set, with dazzling splendor,
and now under it, around it, and upon it,
we spread the hay to say:
we remember.
Our Lord was born in a milk cow's cave
and a horse's stable.
In poverty, simple and humble
He came to love and save us,
and so now we, in humility'
come to this table, as to a stable,
to celebrate His birth.
Mother then gave me a loving look
And I knew what she meant me to say
"Christ is born" I boldly proclaimed,
and equally bold, all replied.
With a stab of pain I missed my father.
My Mother then slipped from her seat
and with Holy Water gave us each a blessing.
Now I don't want to brag, but I have say
that again I knew, what I had to do
and I prayed the prayer for our family,
asking God to give us health and happiness,
but all of a sudden I didn't know what else to say
so I gave the stranger a pleading glance
and he turned to the icon and continued to pray.

How shall we greet Thee,
High King of Glory and Holy Child?
The angelic hosts hymn Thee,
The heavens give Thee a star,
The shepherds offer Thee their wonder,
The Magi their gifts,
The earth a cave,
and the manger a bed of straw.
In darkness, light is created.
Old things pass away, all things are new.
Thou who hast no mother in heaven,
is now born without a father on earth.
Thou who art without flesh,
becomes incarnate.
The Word puts on a body.
The invisible is seen.
The timeless has a beginning,
The Son of God becomes the Son of Man.
As God thou dost share in the poverty of our flesh,
That we may share in the riches of the Godhead.
The earth is not left without gentleness.
The earth is not left without beauty.
The earth is not left without love.
Slava Boh
Glory to God
Amen

After the prayer ended
we sang the Church hymns for the feast
prayed a blessing for the meal,
and finally sat down.
The stranger took over.
Lighting a candle for Christ
    the light of the world,
breaking the Christmas bread,
    giving us each a piece
    as Christ the bread of life,
and finally offering a toast of wine
    to celebrate the cup of salvation.
Then my mother topped it all off.
Taking a little jar of honey,
sticking a clove of garlic in it,
and giving us each
a honey coated clove of garlic,
gently but firmly making us eat it;
to remind us that life is both bitter and sweet
the honey to sweeten our lives,
and the garlic to keep us healthy.

Finally I got my Bobalky.

18

The place our feast came from
is hard to imagine.
It wasn't a catalogue, store, or computer.
It came from a way of life, and a place.
It came from joys and memories, deep in our bones.
It fed our heart and soul as well as our belly.
The big bowl of Machanka, or Mushroom soup
was cooked from much more,
than sauerkraut, cabbage, and onions.
It simmered from our adventure to the mountain,
Mom and Dad together, with the girls and me,
the thrill of discovering the mushrooms,
the view of the valley out beyond the trees,
our hurrying home in the gathering gloom,
the giggling laughter as it started to rain,
and the triumph we felt when we finally got home.

About this Christmas Eve feast,
four things I would say.
First everyone kept and observed it.
Secondly all agreed it should have twelve courses
   after the twelve apostles
   who were simple men,
   who bore forth the good news of the Gospel
   like the fasting foods of this feast,
   though the humblest foods they be
   announce the birth on earth of God's son.
The third fact of this feast is a truth,
   that is really rather funny,
   namely nearly no one agrees
   on how to keep the feast.
   Traditions  vary from village to village
   and even from family to family.
And the fourth truth is that all of the above
   doesn't matter,
The feast celebrates a life with the earth.
We grew the cabbage for Grandma's Halubky,
our Baba's famous cabbage rolls,
and we planted, hoed, and dug the potatoes,
which she whipped up and served hot, with herbs.
We grew and ground the grain she used
to bake the breads and roll out the dough
for her wonderful wee pirohy.

Now the stranger told of faraway places,
  while we remembered events and adventures
  as we ate our way, one after another,
along the menu of twelve courses.
Quickly the night grew darker and deeper,
so we bundled up, to carol our way,
down the hill, past neighboring farms,
and on through the village to Church.
    Then it happened again.
    I suddenly thought of my father,
and the stranger seemed to read my mind.
He laid a gentle hand on my shoulder and said:
"God hears your prayers.
Your father will soon be home,
for the fighting has passed to a far away land,
and the front is now far from our border."
    No sooner had the words left his mouth
than a caroling crowd appeared
like the choir of angels on Bethlehem's hill
to trumpet the news of this holy night.
Now In swelling song we moved along.
Many of us then, couldn't read or write
but we could sing all through the night
from the carols and hymns in our heart,
and every Christmas we did so.

On the way to the Church,
we met some Shepherd Carolers
who following a time honored tradition
were dressed like shepherds
with sheepskins wrapped around them
accompanied by angels in long white robes
wearing tall white hats
like those we imagined that angels wore.
Together this troupe built a manger scene
with all of the holy figures
that they carried as they caroled.
When they came to a house
they would put on a play
with each shepherd in turn
kneeling before the manger
and reciting his rhymed part of the story,
of the birth on earth
of the Christ , the king of Glory.
In-between with the angels
wondrous carols they'd sing
and at the end they would bless the house.

Well kids,
Christmas for us
had its heart in the Church.
With a blaze of candles,
the darkness was overcome.
With everyone singing,
the silence was broken.
And with all the families gathered
from the village, hills, and valleys,
all loneliness was squeezed out
by the warm embracing hug of belonging.
The meal had blessed us
through the gifts from creation.

Now in our Church and service
we smell prayers perfume from the incense
we hear our faith sung and chanted
we view it on walls and icons painted,
and from the chalice we taste it.
Wrapped in the love of God and neighbors
we partake of a world that is beyond
and yet here, so near, and real.

Oh! But I almost forgot the end of the story.

When I got home with the stranger, late in the night, or early Christmas morning, my mother came to say "Good Night", and she whispered to me that she had been desperate, and prayed for God's help to give her children a beautiful Christmas, and her prayer had been answered.

In the morning Mother asked the stranger if he would pose for a picture with the family before he left and he agreed. We said "Good bye" and never heard from him again. We sent the film away to be developed and when it came back about three weeks later the photo looked like this.